Where
the
Arrow
Falls

Where the Arrow Falls

DAVID WEVILL

TAVERN BOOKS
PORTLAND

Copyright © 1973, 2016 David Wevill.

All rights reserved.

Printed in the United States of America.

Cover art: Rebecca Clark, *Bird 5 (Awake)*, 2013.
Graphite on paper. 10.5 x 8 in.
Copyright © Rebecca Clark. Courtesy of the artist.

David Wevill, 1935-

ISBN-13: 978-1-935635-59-8 (paperback)
ISBN-13: 978-1-935635-60-4 (hardcover)

LCCN: 2016930160

Originally published by Macmillan in 1973.

FIRST TAVERN BOOKS EDITION

98765432 First Printing

TAVERN BOOKS
Union Station
800 NW 6th Avenue #255
Portland, Oregon 97209
www.tavernbooks.org

For Shan

We have lost our natural images. All the images we make are twisted, hammered, brilliant. But the complexity of our time is a fiction, like Dante's dark wood. We must find the trail that runs through it, our senses become extra persons walking beside us. That is not to deny the self but to increase it. The increased self is not the figure of man attached to all other men in a carcass-strewn web of dead and living relationships. He is alone as he ever was and perhaps that is not bad. Perhaps he should not try to communicate but to himself. He must learn not to lie to himself before he can not lie to others. Our literature is full of striptease, learning aloud and confessions of failure, invitations to touch in others what we do not want to touch. It looks like truth, but it is the big lie that facts make truth. If there is a truth it is a total fiction, a gigantic metaphor encompassing all. In which, if the parts naturally fit, it is all right. The lesson in Genesis is that there is a way we ought to think in order to survive. Our fiction is that this is not enough. Our gods are the unaccountable, uncontainable facts, the flies in the ointment. We are afraid of the thought of the full circle: not as the Hopi were, who left the design unfinished so the soul could escape: but because the full circle would free us from the trivia we have become addicted to. What we need are allegories so harsh and simple that they will dissolve the objections of what they fail to contain, and free us to think in natural and not artificial terms. Then the politicians will be forced to lie in a new way we can perceive, therefore they will come to question whether their lies are worth it. And it will not be, on either side, the cant of violence and war: which are ways of breaking out of the circle only to enter a smaller one. By natural metaphors I mean, those which are necessarily part of the world, not those which we have added for our convenience as ways of saying "I am." McLuhan has perceived a wrong turn, and described it. He must be a worried man; but his disciples are not, they do not see the turn as wrong, they see that it relieves them of all future obligations to intervene as other than wires buttons and eyes. This system is not the kind of circle I mean. If McLuhan-man can spend a month in the Arizona desert without his gadgets, then return to his gadgets unbeaten, he is a better man than I thought. A man who can do that can conceive the kind of circle I mean. This may be why Jesus went into the wilderness, to think. It is our unrelieved addiction to one sort of thing that kills us, not the dilemma of alternatives, not the attempt to live two lives, or many lives, within the circle. The prophets after all demanded blood, and fear, and pain, not a swaying with the times. In our day that which is hardest may be the most natural, the most simple: it is easy to be complex, one just is. But complexity releases an arrow toward unity: the sacrificial victims of our day, scattered, dismembered, psychotic, live in our blood, crying for some target. Our inventions are angels dancing on a pin. I like those angels, but wish they were larger and the pin a mountain. It is all so subcutaneous, so hypodermic. Where has the air gone. Into my bladder where it hurts. I mean the big air. In my lungs where it hurts. What does not hurt. I do not know or care, I hurt. How to get rid of the hurt. Love me. What if I cannot love you.

That is not possible because if you understood you would see I am really very lovable. What if I neither see nor understand. Then you are not being honest. What if I see and understand and do not love you. Then you must be feeling threatened, by something inside you. What if the threat I feel is you. That is not possible, I think of myself as a child, I can do no harm but am harmed by others. But the threat I feel comes from you. I don't want to talk about it any more please. We have lost our natural images. How can we make a lyric of the world we do not know. Because I need light to write this by, a whole landscape must die to serve a coal mine. I could have waited till daylight.

PART
1

1

The top of your head is still open
fragile, hearing whispers of the sun

your teeth are early and strong
your birthmark grows
a rose, in the small of your back

your eyes are smoky and dark
the lashes longer than ours

your rage
knots you so
I can't untie you

all in all you're a fine one
your strength in Leo but jammed between
Aquarius and my fish

soon you'll be a year
our trees are full of owls
our chimney full of young swallows

fire and water and air
and the earth is yours to grow on

meanwhile you have no friends

2

I buried the dead
baby rabbit
found under the cedars
under the cedars

it lies in the ash-pit
flattened by rain
perverse blue of the flies
has gone to haunt another wind

my daughter, blind
to what small life
death can happen   Here is a mind

of daybreak and sunset cliff
and an acre of trees
give shade in place of water
Here I learn my time is longer than suns

that, by seeing, by
giving I return
through the back ways of god dragging
my heart like a smashed placenta

sticks leaves dust
out into the open, as
the rabbit trailed its—

break me, I say, break me but do not
scatter the parts
they were a long time growing they
learn to love, painfully, at the end

3

For the Sangre de Cristos
where they appear
fifty miles before the eye can see them

—the eye, blind
from desk and midnight lights   I happened on Cortes
lying under a pinon tree
muttering "Land, my land"

                                        Here
his children come
come, before they are broken
or come, by being broken
to break against the sun or the long moon
drying her vulva among the pine needles

Dark night
her vigil
kept by skunks

                                        or her vigil kept
by angels
lashing their wings to the treetops
each tree a halo pointing to blood dawn

No   no crucifixion
no more crucifixions
man of blood

the mountain breasts are full of milk
milk of black and the soul a solitary tree
for the panther, for who moves
softly here   One among us

or us
in the figure of One
so the sky is once again the jay's nest
and the worm flies in its song

4

Hurt
by our hurt

because we could not
share or be her

a hole
where her body had been, now
imagining it

like scatterings of salt

needing an ocean to
be...

        what is
the whisper that heals
from our dandelion lives plucking
their promises, petal
by petal

—I have seen the bone too,
I ran, being afraid

believe us   there is death in it
and whatever life is there
may be yours, not ours

but   because we could
not, what

is, is,
and there you were

without

and here the crows attend you
our smiles like flashes of tin could not defend you

more
than the earth

5

the candle fixed in a black room
will seem to move
left and right

under the delusion there is
an American Voice

explanation, eating the past
prediction, feeding the future

classical mechanics
got us to the moon...theories
evolve, and we are incomplete...

if Nature is the set of all
observations...if

theories are instruments
for making predictions about
observations, the

cool sudden death of the mountains

had you no faith

in the sun's return...who
wills him to suffer, and her

we are still a great way from that star
of new man, and
despite these visions
matter screams under time

as these hills of Mexico
grind an old man's drunken tears to dust

and the yellows the blues
the gold the crimson
eat out the heart from my figure of night

					January 1971

6

His look, they said
would melt mountains

the mountains are still there, the
ghost of Crazy Horse
still dances visions, stone

impenetrable stone
keeps nothing out

and this poet gets his bang
from repeated annihilations
        falling through time like a stone
to the
one
word

absolute

importance
is nothing alive
the air, before and after man, so pure
a stone never carved

it is wistful to play at God

and murder the living in your dreams

7

hero must break with his mother, be
pure energy there-
after. So
in a dry summer
the cedar tree becomes a torch...pouf!
And his words, dishonest, because partial
(as Mao is a functional lie) must
                            free him from gravity
to complete
his *physical* vision, in transcendence

no cat can be a hero
being too lithe in their dance

there's fear in the cardinal too
his red precedes the jaybird's blue
and still, the foetus with two legs
wingless, is the beggar

       I lay and slept
       the hour of my birth
       dark as the stone's throat
       crying into flower

purple that
of the unborn eye
moving around me

night of the people I'd known

love of their unknowing
in this tomb of insolence
crying one name

the poet, the poet's wife
up a long tunnel of twisting water
born before me, after me

lilies of rain
suddenly all over
child-white in the wind that breathed them

under, down
dark gentians toward
the night unborn

dry-mouthed, I rise from my mother
to say her life will bloom again
is not to know that

or she who wrote the poem about

the small dead deer, crying
to her words like a child to her dolls
have no country, want none

is all a film, here
broken, there melted, by
too hot a light...or run too
slow (for effect) to survive
a second or third showing...the sun
that burns away all permanence...kills

what
can replace
the center. I speak of the heart. These words
(heart) returning in the simplicity through
the trail of breakages of a long ago series of
years (dead in exile). Now
intermittent as news of Vietnam, repressed
wanting to know no more.

Caring, unspeaking

a house
broken of its mother

who is to time
what seed

to the apricot tree
was.
                Gesar of Ling
tumbled his flaming horse from the clouds
of heaven, came

the way of the nagas,
killed monster
                    returned. Now heaven

is throated with jets...
the hero on wings carries a hundred souls

as Jesus rose in epiphany
over Dorval
                  that winter, or seemed
in the snow-light

someone real:
                more mother than man

And I cannot move forward from these
not to your love, though I love you

must try my self against stones
or clawing from anus to mouth
repeat the journey I slept

slimed with my own birth
at the edge of dawn, where sun breaks
and the keen pain of the knife

cuts twice

8

At night or just before dawn
dogs in the valley
baying, up the loose stone road
                invaded our hill
a deer? light hoofs
broke the woods' edge
before the wild night mouths
                that broke my dream
melted to echo
the nightmare
                the blood chase
hungry, always hungry
and the bones of the hills glowed
in the afterlight
                the river
under a red unrisen sun
or a red unsetting moon
                in the small hours
when time returns
and the stone breasts of the hills
suckle the deer to their deaths
                or to mine: foretold by the heart's
hoofs leaping
the loose stone road

breaking the woods' edge—
deer-self, deer-self!
                      ahead of the dogs
all windows open like eyes
                            and the stars closed
knowing now
not archetype or dream
but the breaking lungs and heart—
and the forest alone is safe—the forest alone!

9

Somewhere
there is a woman trying
        to teach herself her self

do you say you love her
all the doors
slam on a single hinge

                Ophelia
where are you
I have your hair-ribbons
        not mine, not mine

I have a date with my father
all gifts come and are taken away

they dragged the pond
they found her

ever since then her death has been
a vision, her smile
        like a pained cross
asking

for water
more water

or is it blood

10

There is no equality among those
who suffer. Tones come through
into the bones of the ear, we

hear crying, the
depth of the crying is unknown but
as light changes, we feel it:
the light before rain
                    the light after rain

Love
cannot redeem this. Torn
from its light, the eye knows nothing but pain,
though the light is pain, you
could not touch the pain
in your daughter's eye but

find a jungle. Those
who must live, cannot live
easily. What breaking point—
when the sun spread its talons and fell
on her playroom: fire
feathers blood her father's eye

We must be
fanatics even to breathe. The
quiet ones more so. Cold
as the sharp-shinned moon over
the cedars. It
is alone.

11

April six.
My sister is born today.
Our family never spoke, I
do not speak now.

12

Who are you, I ask
or have stopped asking

must we begin
a body-count among friends

and is pride such a fashion
you wear people like clothes

—spezzato, shattered
the faces you see

even in mirrors. Broken one,
she needs more than your

passion. Give her the energy
of the quiet, the very still

You may smash faces
but not the stars

Lean your flame on her head.
She is your only moon.

13

As I grow older
I lose that fire
that left these scars,
new music in my ears

Now I dance for the sake of play
but be careful: this
too is a phase, old
matter can return...said

the goat who sang the mass
watching Goya paint
the last face, his hand
not broken like his mind

the bleating shadows
the bad breath of the starved
there is still a Duchess of Alba
A white pretender to God

14

As people dreamed
of shipwreck, now
planes crash nearby, in a mothlike flame
               or owl wings: there
are never survivors

in a flight of five jets
one folded its wings
and fell

I woke with fire on my skin
it was dawn: a
               swallow beat on the fire screen, black
and white of old ash. I
opened the door, it planed into the wind

and the young ones in the chimney
cried for food—
I am not milk or worms
               your mother will come

but the air
seemed waiting: my eyes, winged with flame
flew over the trees

                    hunting for victims, heat
to body's heat, the soar
of ash settled to cloud
the sun did not rise

someone, somewhere, gone
my bed is a swamp, and I lie
draining into the lost bones under me

it is late and the world is old

in the word "beginning" I hear no end

15

The birds of terror
were golden and red.
They flew idly
over the green-blue delta.

What were they looking for.
A couch with a lady
naked, reclining. A man
returning from harvest with his gun.

It seemed
they were blind.
The black of the jungle whispered,
night-birds.

But one turned, with a cast in its eye
white as pearl; or the eye
of a farm-boy
made to study

fiction. And suddenly
was on me, like
a spiderweb, my
rifle wilted.

But passed as a ghost
through my bones. Or as though
I were the air cells become
when violently killed.

I would start here.
This is nobody's war.
But dreaming the scar of that beak.
Those feathers entered like splinters.

Child, child, father, mother.
Death of the womb and womb's fruit.
I cannot pity.
I cannot love.

16

Cottonmouth
dead
with a hole
in your side

flies at the closed mouth
flies at the hole
even now
I wouldn't touch you

olive, with rusty bands
the slit eye
only a picture of watching

broken S
shape in the stony dust
far from water, where your bite is worst
in death, venomous still
as ripped from the living

—Pilinszky, patient Hungarian
I have your papers on my desk

to try and bring you alive

this day the snake died
in this dust, Harbach
cripple

venom
in memories...stones
of dry Texas, not

those dark potato fields
where prisoners crept

between wires hung with scorpions
and daybreak, the spirit's release

into no new world

17

Drink water
eat stone
build with tree
fish with bone

city
smelling of new glass
putty, drying cement

the sun will mark a new
turning (too many
mistook glass doors
for daylight)

                    hunger
                    and thirst
make daylight
divisions of the clock
across the land

in my time zone
I hear an older sun

a baby tells its dreams

directly to God

we must go to Yucatan
to find what gods were?

as the poor wake still
in lands that feel hunger and thirst

my love, my complex love
we move to discover ourselves
in silence, only

no one comes

and our selves
do they go with them, stay
from us like broken
masks, the seen
and the hidden face

possessed
by those we hide from

with whom
we ate and drank
with whom
we built and might have

fished

                water
                stone
                tree
                bone

old glass
old cities
old cement

and the sun broken in a million eyes

18

West over dry rivers
the smell of dead earth

only men of bones could
ride here, live here

did: and are now gone
the brown and the sunburnt white

where there has been such dry
death, the land is long to recover

may the wind blow my seed
where there is shade and water

may the wind blow my eyes
where the bones lie, that are harder

than mine, or my kind
a hell not walled by glass

who went the journey to grass through
each others' blood, and died of it

out there
in the mirrorless dust

saw no false hope or face
but their own, a mirage at the end

19

America is so hungry
space is hungry
the sea is thirsty

America drinks the sea
and eats the land and
bites at space

now as a wolf
now as a bird
now as a serpent

all voices of the dead sing
the hunger of America
dreams mattered once

dream
and the dream's teller
mattered once. Now

in the dream museum
fox skin and bison skin
serape and moccasin foot

return
on their pale wearers
the blood voice mutters prayers

we have not earned. But
we are hungry
we are thirsty

save us, O teller
give us the key to the heart
piss on our cardiograms

they are false maps
sing us a truer
falsehood, sing

of rivers and stones in the blood
before we have eaten the land
before we have drunk the sea

before we drift
into the tides of space

for we cannot return

20

Not Navajo
you don't count

not the child
of a Maya god
you have no name!

wanderer: where are the lives
you have put behind you

the mask
torn from your face
tears flesh with it

where in the whirl is the self
blood-of-bone, though you

may dance and speak
with tongues of the older dead
who are you? what

gift but your loss
do you bring

to the listeners
under
the hill—

Maya, Navajo
Yaqui, Hopi, Tlingit, etcectera

those sleepers
deep
beneath your fjords and farms

your city's
secret arrowhead

its closed
bloody
eye

21

Stravinsky
farmed the air
        for thunder
rattle of coins
in a tin cup—
        rain
on Broadway, the curse
of music
        reinventing the ear

is dead. And the ear
will be slow to catch him
        percussion of drummer bones
nerves of roller-coaster suns

I am the skeleton
of risen Dionysos
        frail fairy bones
dance
in a carnival century
        glued to wires—

repeat me
try and repeat me!

22

Beginning now say
this is a year of drought, and
        rain must follow our words
but
wheat dies, the
"beautiful surviving bones"
pity India
not us

There was a time I thought I was part
of disaster. I
have seen nothing, I
        am an eye moving, back and forth
round and round
the spiral of birth, talking

Rilke: am not
the same person I was...
        why write to my friends?
inevitable
burden of love. Flaw
in the luminous world-mind.
Fish-thrash.
Guilt.

One humanity. One time. One heart.
Beginning now, say
        the rain will come
and I will take
the identity of rain and
dance with my sisters and brothers!

forgive. I cannot melt.
There was a time I thought I knew death
too: where the mouth
        with stones for teeth
ate at my dreams
and I sat in a blind room
carving models of clay
        others, for sacrifice

or lay in the cloud
playing a solitary flute...
I was not a poor man in Peru

Death of a tree
in this page. Your long legs
crush the grass. You move
slowly
        with bent head, nun
of nature. The natural wind.

I am doing it all wrong. This is
music, I want
words cold and stubborn-born
        to eat like flame crystals
under the skin. What
nerve remains.

When the baby cried
in the psychiatric ward
all the attendants came running—
        the baby was sane

her egg
was barely cracked. I
hold her like a violin
tenderly, talking her sounds. Forgive

my melting.
Beginning now, say
this was a crystal year
        blood of soldiers
returns
to furnish us. What. That the old
die in their beds. That the beds be prepared.

23

Find
a country you love
a place, a people
        not you

ride their wild horses
share their rice
suffer their famines

the acid sun
risen above sand
will bleach you like their
ghosts
        your words
        your feet
will dance and sing
a memory of now

            you, you

here, smoke
on the wind
        the eagle fades
        his feathers die

but
voices cry from dust

you think
you know those tongues

you know
you've dreamed their skins

still the heart
or vision dies

24

The old words
sag, like muscles

where does the heart
keep more

I hear you know about
witchcraft—

for money
I'll tell you their names—

the prostitution song

the ear
faithful to mouths
I have lost my song
Sell me your song

my song returns
why do your songs die

they live in the sun
they have no shadows

the heart is both

up
and down
and wide as the eye sees

forgive
a cross-eyed man

25

i

To the east
above the river
still-shadowed cliffs

whatever happened here
is always here. Sun

crosses them
and over the grass toward
sunset (not yet) my
mind moves

ii

It is ready now, said Taiowa
for human life, the final touch
to complete my plan

and then the slamming waves
and curl of outboards
dead echoes in living riot

sunflash like guns
on bodies fighting the wind

the
snakes left, then the trees
the fishes went

It is very good
said Taiowa,
destroy it

iii

I dream of magnesium destroying my friend
and this woman stretched
like a pelt, blue bruise
where cunt was

                 in the moon
we turn to shadow
I blend with you, you blend with me
and go north into the sky
devoured by roc or condor

the grass was never ours

whatever happened here

was not to us, but its memory
reads our fate

                in the sun
our bodies return
blackened with smoke of time
to walk alone by the river
hand in hand with the wind, which

is always here

iv

The square is
completed, this
is the fifth world, where

knowledge is too old to scream

or the heart too weak—

abstract
like the pattern of a blanket
and still
they jailed them in Washington
veterans, many

the birdbaths

of America
well over with tears

abstract—
what we do with our minds
was once an animal running

an asylum of savage gestures
making the curled-up body
this much child

as flame can
or the coming of slow dawn

V

Whatever happened here is always
happening. Eagle and hummingbird
dance the air we've
crashed, fire
is our scorn for the living

—break it, said Taiowa
each world is complete
each world is less than the first
learn to live with less

or you will have nothing

and the mockingbird mocks
in the lightning-cracked tree

26

autumn in spring

        what does happen after
a long night: of
cities we cannot repair again, dark
roads, red rivers
        the Cheyenne stumbling north
through autumn blizzards
dead as the figures on cards
        kings, and queens

what does
happen to the mind
        waking in cloud
burned by dreams, no
less self than the wary deft-
handed body gardening stones
        this Wednesday, the sun
a fiery negative

come mask
and be the season you pretend
our lives
are photographs we cannot burn

let heroes
know who they are, their
false selves wake them at night
to find no new image in the
      horror that killed a people, no
dead tongue, no living dream

I rode the horse into spring
the cloud and thunder mare
      with a lame leg
but the hills were autumn, autumn brown
there was no fear and no pain

but I imagined I was alive again

27

Not only me
this silence, you
know the wind I speak of
has no direction

not the skeleton, we
are not windows for
seasons or birds
to pass through. Yet

this is the illusion,
oak, the vine
has killed my lower branches—

bitter for friends, their eyes
startle
things I do not
know I say

but my spine is not
straight with the earth:
stomach, heart, throat
brain and crown of head

walk crookedly. I
return to the seed-self
made less
by this one life

lived, already
in ignorance.
We must think

who we are

        think
not of our own
perfection, or
dream of the other faces
coals of an old fire

that burn
and burn the nerve
so these words for you
come as smoke over a prairie

or fall as ash
over a city
without
sun.

        We
are two years old
our child is almost one, let
that, in yet another year
of war

be enough. It is not
our blood, this wind, it
thins us like corn. Our despair
is helpless

our silence
remembers words, strains
against the glass that birds
smash dead against. What

talks to us
talks as a god
hurt by our anger. Once a year
our friend goes underground

she returns, yellow as corn
with her dreams
written. So the dead
used to return

in pain along the sun's track

to earth. From birth
the four directions
are confused. I

do not know why
you love me, but
there was once
a child...

28

    The voices that cry against war
lack humility. The poet is no longer a
solar creature, the sun rhetoric
won't do. Nor is the poet
pelagic, he is polluted
with the ocean. He
must know himself...Proteus,
elusive but effective...
He goes where he will.
He does not speak for the world.
A mirror of the self that mirrors the world.

By this
coming through
the maze, so
the four journeys
may be completed

time
both near and far. I
love my lost friends
        so my dreams tell me
the four ways
lead to the center

there is
no break

and courage may be
to *wait*
till the black wasp
finds my web, and stings

and the skin hangs
drying in the sun, the legs
curl and the abdomen shrivels

the terrible love
of the black wasp
searching the home
and killing the spider
(the maze won't trap
his folded wings)

turn back at the oceans
turn back at the poles
you have not yet
found your home

        but dream
you have?
our half a hill—

this is a point, a beginning

from here
the journey

not restless
but drawn

like a bow
aimed at beyond

29

He asks each sunrise
for a new mask
to be worn until his
face can take the sun

       habit, habit
gone in the nights
lost, like dogs
so the fumbling of his hands
savages things

even
when light
is clearest—

this black one hangs in the hall
it is a gift, like his others

no one
completes its phase: they
       grow inward and vanish, crying
names
he cannot give them: they
want someone, are mates of light
weeping elsewhere

ii

      they are a crowd
come to no
event, random
as a leaf pile
dark faces of a Sicilian funeral
bright faces on the Padre Island sand
conning shells
this
stalling of the mind—

why will he not choose one
and wear it?

iii

By noon the number of the day
is a continuous thunder,
the black mask has no body
but has become what it can see
inward, and trees,
cedars, circle the wooden shed
waiting for the cry "Eureka!" or "Fire"
to come as the wind climbs
                higher and higher

and sun
crawls the cliff
like diamondbacks...the
unrepentant rocks are his bones too
his back bends with the river
old fishbones put on flesh
and dance his eyes two circles
the holes in the middle are night
his mouth is a widening song

one by one
his fingers put out leaves, searching
for airs they have not touched...this
is where Hamlet falls
where Little Wolf shot Thin Elk through the heart

iv

the last is human
to bear the blood of others
through the mask's eyes
where no holes were carved

to give or take
pain

"in my life
too little compassion"
—his father

what then

comes of knowing his trees
more faithful than friends
his animals
less so

      the mask is mad
its madness is black, it
grips night and shakes it

it is hungry for the face it hides

V

at night came the storm
at daybreak the shaken rocks
hung loose from matted holes
there was smoke on the wind
a glitter in the grass

he cried for the mask to come

and touch him to his feet
five fingers climbed his backbone, hooves
of elk multiplying
expert at silence

where were the caves of the storm
hiding, a
city aware of its end, an
iron bridge no longer above its river, the
mask's eyes, black lava

wept centuries too far back
old smoke, old fires, old rain
she touched him with these fingers
he got up dragging her hand
to the fire and held it there

vi

his trouble
his having no face

his having eyes

but no face
like anything that watches
is unknown, whole

of the whole earth
but nothing, mask

speak to her kindly
and not of the stars

his soul is a clam
in a borrowed shell

by night
the faces have gone

his true face multiplies through all
the deaths it comes to

asking, asking
to be seen

as God
was once

in a
corn seed

30

Goddess of the city dump
old woman of no age, her dogs, her
chickens, bits she has gathered to sell

she keeps no mirrors
the dump reflects her face
the earth would find her
too tough a thing to swallow

over the dump swarms
the creator, a million wings
that lay their eggs in her

and she is the cradle of the coming
god, from her weeping sores
the babe is born, whom
we have hidden

ants, lice, flies, and the scorpion
stingers of day and night
day's print, night's negative

make her a sentimental song
tell her we love her, Maria

we shit on you, we
shit to forget you

picture of our mothers
of earth repeatedly raped, locked
in the mad ward, time no object

no name, no children now
but a face of catted stone
and when she dies her
chickens will peck her eyes

her dogs blunt their teeth
from hide to bone, her
death will seem quaint in our day, an

"original" has left us, one
we can smile at, as the surviving earth
teems with her winged children
breaking our sleep at dawn

on the Mekong, the Rio Grande

31

Bly came: his serape
hung like a suit of armour
            his hands
weaving apocalypse whirled
a ghost of America into the snarling

present: voice
cracked with anger
            —was it an act? Those
pale eyes
        paleface profile
that placed the Minnesota nights
in words delicate as fox-tracks in the snow

—the journey Trickster made
also disembowled him
        glasses
winked like mask-eyes: body went
then mind became
            a slush of simplicities, back, back
to what daylight asks
and bad dreams fulfill

I remembered this quiet man

and now hear noise: one
        hubris replaces another so
man can live, how
long?

When stones join the wind
it is time to go underground
to visit our brothers the ants

to live with the smallness of things, be
sure of details, wait

32

Then comes the screaming dog
his tail on fire   face
of my father   over the grass he
sets smoking

it is dark   his body
lies burning where it fell   Trees
kneel over the grass
mound   I am a child
looking   I see
grass but no fire no body no dog no face

ii

Sure, sure he was here
right there! You can hear the wind
a mile away from the top of the valley, vultures
brush the treetops, wind
comes home

                        This picture
needs a woman. Brown
weed in the day-green water, river

asking the cliff for more sun

cold, cold water

iii

And he has become
the thin tail of the fish. Who
kept me half my life is now my child

She? are both one eyes
his hazel mixed with her blue
that is the river color running
through limestone

                                            ...fiery dog

you burnt me

it is dark
trees bend to the river listening

no grass no fire no body no dog no face

33

My friend wants
a "new reality." What
of the old?
There are others

                I breathe

air that is
newly real   I open my eyes on old dreams
and new sunlight

but I am afraid
of the machine in desire, the
                "will to create"
not the will to find

words always fail the ego

to the quiet, words come
as a kind of listening

they are not here
before the wind that brings them

34

"the other hand
from the opposite end of space"

dark/white
eye
of unopened flower

I am morning. I come
slowly. There
is love when I open. There
is no love when they say
"It will open"

My skin will forgive your blood.
Not before death

Yes. Before death.
Before my death seeds your death

helicopter
over stars' peak
        searchlight moon
streaked with feathers

black and white
blood is the break between hands, this
        stone is cold until held
this heart lifeless

35

Last night with Lawrence
page after page
mindless eyewitness accounts

dead people
talk about a living man: his
chairs   his forest   his
view from the Villa Mirenda

over the aching poor
and the vine country
their eyes track silence back
                to a lost voice

they must keep still
to do this: on
foot like pilgrims   feet
in the tracks of the lost fox

the phoenix will cry at noon
tired as he was
he followed no one

they follow him now

like polite dogs trained to obey
to catch   but not to kill

hounding him   hounding him
they who are always too late
that generation   or this or the next
collectors of others' voices

collage of human skin
I spit in your sensitive eyes
I was no Christ that could heal

36

The mountains turn out red hearts
to the sun, rising and setting

a highway paces the wind
we return to our land

still unbroken

ii

A prayer before a journey

the painted desert touch
our pale skin with its colors

the mountains lift their horns
they smell us coming

we are inert: the world moves

iii

behind us we leave

rivers bouldered with dead

in the rising sun it is their blood
that drowns us

in the rising wind their voices
make us listen

forked tongue of snake and rifle
morpheus of polaroid eyes

probes for the hole in the heart

iv

such as we leave is left
without eyes to wander the sun's
track, crying nowhere

such as we've known becomes
the boulders the mountains turning
their red hearts out to the sun

unbroken, indifferent

such as we leave are rivers
returning to their fish: the dark brown weed

of mother entrails, deep
and deeper yet

V

I say good night to all the creatures of fear
they will return

my pale skin takes color from the rocks
I am dressed in splendor

leave me. I know this desert
I turn my red heart out to the pale mountains

I will walk in the sun

37

A man
put together from
several dreams, none his own

stone ovens
empty in the sun
earth ovens smelling of old bread

some, they
cut off the left foot
others enslaved, raped, ran naked

hand in hand
through the ghost dance
of eyes in broken windows

sun sun
come again
bring more life than summer rain

the earth
is hard and strong
you too, if you can bear it

not among the pine of Cibola
or the snow peaks of Lincoln,
beauty the force that endures

saeta
from tree to eyes
in long red skirts, picking herbs

good night
to every thing

and if the night was kind

good morning too

38

Welcome
        to the long wind
                the sheep
scattered over grasses of dust

dry ocean, once
the dinosaur's home
gift of our fathers to you

In the night: this dream
I walk in the shape of a tree
dragging my stone-caught roots
                step by step
towards water: I
am new-born and need milk, I
cry a tree's cry
in the silence of the canyons

the birds put holes in my bark
they too are thirsty
        the sun drinks all
the giver of life drinks all

the dead storm leaves its rain

I drink
and am grass in the valleys
a billion shadows, not one

come the sheep
comes man to my mouth...
I have come of age, and am no one

dust and the long wind

my women gone to the sky
my men are dead or lamed

the names I cry are dead names

in the night
this dream:
a broken hive of bees
a swarm of venom in search of flowers

and the flowers
like Japanese crabs
with faces on their backs

who knows the long wind
or the purpose of agriculture

do the rocks
does the sea

live now
dream then

to have both you must starve on the hill

39

Juniper you stand in the west wind
dry old man of the high plains

so dry
the air is fire
so old
half of you is dead

holes in you the birds have pecked
like dead eyes
gnarled against the weather
your hair falls at a touch

you were our only shade
you stopped what little wind you could

we spoke to you in the night
our closest neighbor
the moon took on
your shadow from the sun

now it is time to go

I touch you like a son

your dry white flank
knows nothing but heat cold wind
father tree

now you are alone in our eye
now you are alone on the land

our dust flies east to cities

40

Red rock wall
the navajo blue sky
dry with locusts of dust

we touch
at our wettest points
in the cool camp of cottonwoods

no rivers but yours and mine
survive the hanging sun

clothes off
in the bramble of fire
flesh softer, thinking of rock
                fingers of quick water
here, to this place
a dance where wildcats lived

suddenly together

and there is death
and we are free, but
think of the clamp of fire and steel
                on darker skins

violent history
flows from the soft tip and cunt

into sand like blood

body so easily broken
no sun was ever tender to you
you do not grow in peace like grass
the sun hates rivers

hates our blood

41

I see a face in the stone
because you say
there is a face in the stone

also I saw
an angel in her, because
she said: there is an angel in me

and I willed it

now there is nothing but
a memory of a face and an angel
this hot morning
without wind

ii

Last night they shot me
but I got up
and ran to a lake
but the lake was dry

I passed a pony

running thirsty
he had a red wound
on his flank, from the sun
he whinnied, he
thought I had four legs
the lake was a dry red bed
I do not know where the water had gone

iii

This is a country
of deep lies
the face in the stone, the angel
the pony, the dry lake

but the wound
bled, I
feel it today in the sun

and the voice of the pony
mistaking me for its kind, the
wound in me, the
wound in its flank, was bleeding

iv

I do not know who was shooting
who drank the lake dry who
carved the stone who
made her an angel

but
there is time to learn
why I came to the this place, why
I was running, and who were the others

I cried to warn
not to come closer
not to come closer

my tail was on fire and my mane

42

You turned, she
was standing behind you
she cried to you and you waited

she started hitting you
with the stone fingers of one hand
until your forehead bled

—when the pain was too much
you knocked her down—
"Isn't that what you wanted?"

why
does she keep returning
with her eyes of dried tears

to remind you that hell is blonde
and there is no heaven of children

and no blood can charm to life
those stone white fingers

43

The seeded clouds
scatter their rain in the valley
the rainflowers are out

but the leaves of the oak
crinkle up like clenched hands, it
is unnatural

                        They talk of drought
old men, who know the earth
whose farms return to stone
as their hearts have done

We are strangers
our twenty corn plants
drink water from our hands

rain is a mood in our lives, drought is a mood
for the land was never ours

we are its keepers
now it is frail and old, while we have blood
it can drink, unpoisoned in us

44

questions, assassinations
wet newsprint
scattered through the trees

as Tusayan
they look for signs of their age
in the holes of the burnt kiva

their children would like to inhabit
these ruins, home
is nothing, a
lost key

                I think back
and am not here
thin brown shapes slipping through
the rivers' fingers, hungry for roots
a baby hung at its mother's hip
uncrying, the land will not have it

what did we do
to create this pale terror
to worship the poetry of the crow
as snow falls

Manuelito and Carnera Mucho
torn from their orchards,
an answer replaced by a question,
                death by paper

I say be humble but
know your own arrogance

for to be one with the dead is to be
their God

he walks in shadow
he walks in his own shadow
his shadow which was once the only sun

45

The trees who were buffalo
stand planted, feeding on the ghost grass

a wave of wind sets them running
between mesas like bone cutting through flesh

dies, and they die
mounds of dead brush, humped, no color, still

ii

No shelter but time
speeding through dry rain:
songs for this land, but who sings them?

cicada, snake
the coiled up dance
in supermarkets priced beyond hope
jewels of sky, moon on water

deep eyes
searching the knife in every heart

iii

I saw a foal by its mother
a baby in her father's arms
a lamb tottering to milk

the land lives off itself
my eye is a seed blown wrong
an arrow still twanging for blood

46

These elegies, black dreams
I can't unknot their names
I put my head in their mouths
bite out their tongues
but they speak

night after night
wings of the condor, whistling from high snow
slashing the dead graves
open

dear ones
he did not know
earn or love to the limit of him, what
cried in his sleep was not birds

his ghost-shirt caught in a tree
he smacked the air with his hands
the voices talked him under

let him begin now
give him his daily bread

PART 2

1

I have built you
nothing, what
have I given

distance,
no rest

       no rest
but movement, coming
and going
like the south clouds, over the valley

your eyes

you are waiting for me
but I am here

I think

2

Round and round
the rooms, padding
        on quiet feet

on bed
with your book and bolster, reading
the weather and Lawrence

our nerves make love, we
tear like webs

burn in the late day sun

things here
and absent

3

Quiet as stones, but
unable to weather as stones

our skins
are in love

the crazy jagged colors
or bad dreams, time
gone to the lost, hurt, hunted
ones behind us

there are few
who have stared at the sun
and kept their eyes

mine
or yours

4

Sometimes
the body a god
        sometimes water

sometimes
the eye
its lifetime back through dark

the entrails
congealed in the eye's
        beauty, watching

all that is there
inside and out,
bird complete in its song

but afraid
to fly

5

It is quiet here
no one comes

we wear clothes
for the trees and birds
        not for each other

why then
what do we hide

does blood
show secrets through the skin

or do our soft parts
go masked
        like a god
to keep their power

pure and hidden?

6

When your eye
is in me, I
break

you take
the pieces and
build me a body, no

one I know yet

your lover
my stranger

our child

7

It was so long
and the night
filled with dead faces, crying
to be alive

I found you
in the moon's grave, about four,
some fire you had dreamed
which the black cedars witnessed, kissed

on your body, a live scar
that burned my side

and you
can never tell me

8

We find our selves
as children, but

the masks we wear
come as man and woman

to touch. The child
fades from our eyes

returns as one
who does not know us yet

but in her
the masks will die

a child will return
to both our eyes

9

It is liveliest to be still
listening to some things come and others die

now, when our wills are quiet
breathe as the trees do, without fear

not hidden from man or sun

10

I have built you
nothing, but
our cells know a difference in winds

in touch
a danger

I prayed
to a warped cross, now
I stand half broken, heal me

our cells will melt and close

now is the sun, our moment, given, whole

11

To see it all fresh
forget

bury the bones
then try and find them

hard
harder than death

I am afraid of innocence and
I cannot remember, night
my duty to dream

smells of the wet cedar

my book reads itself
my house is watching me

music out there: rock of the storm
home has eyes
        wind smells of cities
you

forgotten things

drift up in the light
fish-heads without bodies
with living eyes

my duty to dream, not sleep, not
ease like a snake into the hole
of knowing, without eyes

and you are watching
your skin is a number of years
a song I know and don't own

a poem to be found

12

Between midnight and daybreak
seven times for my sins
staring the different winds into their cradles
      owls, nightbirds, cats
the faces I know and do not know—

betrayed by my silence
I think of you now: you burn with me
in this foresleep, before taking your masks and roles
into dreams I cannot control, where
      you triumph or die—
and leave me a husk clinging to a tree

I imagine a better world, larger
a place where the hurt
smile over each others' cradles: dwarf, giant
      twins, the without arms or legs
ones, fat lady and rubber man, Ralph
the man with elephant's legs, the bearded lady—
a family circled by fire
but spared by the other-killing fire

so my head will empty itself
for its own sounds to enter:

the Fool coming late to his hands, an effigy
        of dried shit and straw, that
walks, talks, composes poems
that enter through one eye and out the other
so, in a perpetual circle

adobe man, lost on his own plains
a miracle of nightly resurrection and
daily sleep: Wakdjunkaga, between one birth
        and another, eating his own body, his
night confused with his day: no
enemies, no friends, no god but error

as even the stones   fitted to one another

PART 3

BLOOD CANYON

One of the silent places of the world. The dry white canyon bed, pure sand. Red sandstone cliffs, dark in patches, meeting the sand as sheerly as a wall meets a floor. Under the sand, a foot or so down, it is still wet. The river storms through here in a flash flood, there is a line along the canyon wall where the water runs. Cottonwoods in the narrow coves; tiny farms, and once, long ago, peach orchards. At dusk the angelus of goat bells, hidden around a bend in the skeleton river. Red rock everywhere and sand and a few trees, the rock glowing at night deep ruby as the shadow wells in the canyon like water. A place of dreams. The steep walls are red with blood of its possessors. A hundred years ago, a place of desperation and death. There were the first people, then the Hopi, then the Navajo, each taller than the other; then the little cock Kit Carson with his technique of erasure by fire. To have a dreambed like this canyon where it has all been acted out, a mansion, like a great artery of blood, feeding your sleep forever. "In my father's house..." The Navajo returned. Then the self, long legged and ungainly, looking for a lifeline, anglo man with his body cast in the steel webbing of his dreams. Higher and higher, his blow-torch touches the stars. He is the eagle pinioned in time. It is a frightening place not to belong to, to have known but missed. The silence is that of withheld voices, facts do not fill it. He climbs down and he climbs up, he feels his own sweat, energy running in his legs like a sap from the red rock. But the sun drinks it and he leaves no smell. It is an unconscious woman long past feeling the offense of his rape. A monument to a longer life than his cannibal time. His race came as a bullet aimed dead center at that clock, but the clock had no hands, it kept running. The clock had no machine works but a long memory, unaffected by facts. Try and think like the wind. It is no good. It makes no sense. Because they embodied the created world, all things living and imagined, nothing being dead, the wind was their mind. A continual flux of changing forms bringing them things and taking them away and bringing them back again, without ever losing one thing. We burn out the center of our brains to remember. It is no good. The smell of burning is in everything we touch. The smell is in this canyon, the fire he brings, his own offering. Reduced from the sun to a thin six-foot pyromaniac. It is the smell of his mind. The desire to burn it all down to the one "thing." The alchemist still looking for traces of gold in his burnt hands. Fundamental as hell. And the red rock glows in the dark like a huge coal, burning into his vision, burning out his eyes.

WHITE SANDS

It is the deliberate way the mountains seem to hold back. They blacken in the cloud shadow we are trying to reach, the sun burning our backs from Socorro far behind us. Two hours before sunset everything is heading for supper: sheep, cattle, goats. There's rain about, but it is hard to find it. Two big industrial ranches and a scattered few poor ones with windmills and broken gas pumps. The wheat is two months shorter with the drought. White Sands to the south. Only the mountains seem to know what happens there. Miles of steel fenceline, not the kind ranchers use. The mountains are pulling us east and then south, high pines of the Lincoln Forest, the blue of a thousand miles north. On the right it is all RESTRICTED, like not being able to use the right eye or the right side of the body. So they can cut us in half. They are infinitely secret and important with only the mountains watching them. One imagines missiles stealthing up on moonlit nights, explosions like inverted thunder off there, as if the mountains were put there to hide it. Further east and south is the Plain of Fires, the old lava hills. But at White Sands everything is obliterated because you do not know. I do not want to know: but there it is, paralysis of the right side of my body. The real fear is still the sun. What men do with their minds at White Sands is part of the mad fear of the sun. Or they came without bodies and expect to leave without bodies. No evidence. RESTRICTED. "They were bodiless vapors, playing with fire. They air conditioned themselves out of existence." And so important they have to cut off a fair piece of the earth and set the mountains around it as guards. "Let the people eat science fiction." Melt all the stones, beginning with public statues. In the high mountains of Lincoln Forest, a U.S. Marine Reservation. They make delicate earthenware pots and jewelry, they welcome tourists, permission of The Chief. Somehow their culture survives. Rain now, and livestock on the road. Desert and stones eat the rain leaving only a smell. The secret places of the earth were once sacred. They kept the secrets of spirits, not the secrets of men. Trickster's right hand fought his left hand, wounding it. When he felt the pain and saw the blood he knew he was whole. Perhaps that is the only way back from White Sands. But let it be our blood, not that of our dream-enemies. Or let it pass, like the fenceline on the right, keeping a secret only the mountains know. Our hearts have gone before us, under the cloud, into the mountains. But you feel the earth's wound burning somewhere out there, like a vivisection without an anesthetic, a drop of hot rain on the face. The long steel fenceline watches you safely out of sight. "Go into the mountains. Forget."

"This earth too old, grass too old, trees too old, our lives too old. Then all be new again."

—Arapaho

THE RITUAL

Cawdor rose up from his day bed and shook out his hair. He stumbled to his typewriter. Day rose and fell. By nightfall he had written 300 cantos of his World. A new generation of insects had lived and died outside his windows. The sun from which he took his energy saw many people born and many injured, heard the cries of children and birds. Shadow never moved from Cawdor's house. Others moved in and out, a generation of others, thinking it home. Cawdor was generous with his limited time. It was limited because of World. He did much with his hands and feet, very quickly. He was laying a highway across a void. One worried about the foundations.

Nana did. Nana rose from a dream into a dream. She moved very slowly in the room, a somnolence, hearing the cries of birds and children in her dream. She moved as if the house had no foundations. She felt a generation of insects born living and dying outside her windows. The moon from which she took her energy was hidden during the day, she was left with the sun. Shadow never moved from Nana's house. The sun was too hot, the shadow was too cold. Nana talked to herself. Her words were nerves. She did much with her hands, slowly but very well. She moved subtly, too, and slowly, as if on water or through high grass. One worried about the foundations.

Sometimes Nana and Cawdor met. They met on the dark stairs or in one of the dark high-ceilinged rooms or among the cries of children going up and down as the days rose and fell. There were strangers in the house who had been there for years. They cooked and washed and ate and rose and fell with the days and the cries of the children and birds. When Nana and Cawdor met they talked about love. Love never moved from their house, nor did shadow. They met as the sun and the moon meet in the same sky, one on its way up and the other on its way down. They were glad to see each other. Sometimes children came crying with hurt fingers or in hunger. There was always a stranger cooking at the stove. There was always a stranger with a bandaid or soothing arms, and there was always a child standing in the shadow to be warmed, like a hurt bird, ruffled, out of its world. When this happened Nana or Cawdor or a stranger came and did something. What was done would pass for the time being. The shadow was to blame, or the heat or the cold. Love was very important. One could not do without love in a large cold house that was sometimes too hot. One could not do without the strangers. The strangers needed love and the children needed love and Nana and Cawdor *were* love. So when they talked about love or children or strangers they talked about themselves. What else was there. In a world where things were born living and dying all the time. It was important to keep up valued appearances. Appearances valued carefully enough become the real thing. For Nana and Cawdor this was sacredmost.

Drinking a cup of coffee or eating a plate of spinach the day would begin or end. The strangers would come and stay and go and some were getting quite old. But the house was childlike inside its shadow. There were quarrels, misunderstandings about understanding. Cawdor and Nana would touch. Their hands would break apart and wait to touch again. If someone had a bad feeling he or she would out with it, and something would be done. What was done would pass for the time being.

Cawdor sat in his tower with his manuscripts and telephone and postage stamps and World, which was always lengthening. Nana sat in the kitchen talking or with the cries of birds and children as the heat rose and fell of the day which went by like a film. Sometimes Nana and Cawdor met, on the dark stairs or in one of the dark high-ceilinged rooms. Light crept timidly in through the windows, as if intruding. Every hour of the day was astrologically charted in Nana's nerves. Cawdor did not see the hours passing. He was building his highway across the void. One worried about the direction.

There were accidents, and moments of hopelessness following. Cawdor would bear down on the accident with all his energy, and the accident would cringe, and limp away into the shadow which was always there. But Nana saw the defeated accident waiting there in the shadow, like a hurt child. She loved the accident then and she hated it and wanted it away. If the shadow moved she was watching it. She never missed a movement of the shadow. The shadow was always there and it needed comforting. Sometimes a stranger came with a bandaid or with soothing arms and comforted the shadow. Sometimes the shadow was a child. Sometimes the shadow was in Nana's eyes, but never entirely in Nana's eyes. Nana sent her eyes into the corners, searching. The shadow would become words. That was good. Then the words would turn on Nana and the shadow would move. Then Cawdor would come and the shadow would pretend to die. The shadow was very good at this. It was not deceitful, but the nature of a shadow. Then Nana would smile at Cawdor and Cawdor knew he was strong. Sometimes one worried about the shadow. But never as long as Nana smiled.

There were birthday parties for children and birds and the shadow was always there. Strangers came with gifts and the gifts were opened and put away. At parties the shadow would do a sad dance, and a happy dance. Then the shadow was beautiful. It looked like a child. One worried about the childlikeness of the shadow. The shadow seemed full of life and the love that never moved from the house. Sometimes Cawdor would watch and think the shadow was a child. Then Nana reminded Cawdor that the child was really a shadow and Cawdor would get angry and once more the shadow would pretend to die. Then one did not know whether the shadow was in Nana's eyes or not. Though one knew it was never entirely in her eyes.

Day rose and fell. Some days were better than others and some were bad. On a bad day Nana and Cawdor met frequently on the dark stairs or in one of the dark high-ceilinged rooms and would talk about love. Or on a bad day Nana and Cawdor did not meet at all. Then the house was abandoned to the cries of children and birds and the insects dying in generations outside the windows. Then strangers would come and the talk would be about love. The strangers would wash and cook and eat but really there was no one there. On bad days Cawdor would sit and work on the lengthening World. As World lengthened, the shadow grew. The shadow was then no longer a child, and Nana would sit rocking talking to it, and they would exchange eyes. The shadow's eyes were not the eyes of a child. When Nana wore the shadow's eyes and the shadow wore hers she could see very far. Then the shadow was almost blind. Nana did not fear the blinded shadow. But she was afraid because she knew the shadow would give her back her eyes and want its own back. Nana smiled at the shadow. The shadow did not smile back. Nana wept and the shadow moved closer, groping for its eyes. Then Cawdor came and gave the eyes back to the shadow and Nana's back to her, very reasonably, and the shadow pretended to die. It curled up and slept like a child. This was a good day. But one worried about Nana.

Nana did. She would go away for days and return. Sometimes she would be really gone. At other times she would be there but surrounded by a white nebula of frost, so she was worse than gone. Then one heard the whispering of ants around the walls, voices calling her down. And she moved, a somnolence about a sun whose features were the devil's not Cawdor's. Cawdor did not like this other devil self around whom she moved in her moon-like somnolence. It gave her words. But the words grew slowly budding like children inside her until they were born, like a new generation of children and birds in the dark house. Cawdor waited for the words to be born, one by one, like a patient father. But he did not know the devil their father. Sometimes he would forget and treat the devil-sun-self as he did an accident or the shadow. Only it did not cringe or pretend to die but hung in the house like a horrible halloween while the children talked in whispers. Nana moved through her incubation like one not really there. It was her underground time and damn Cawdor's spade. So Cawdor went up into his tower and lengthened World. This was difficult for all. One worried about Cawdor then.

Sometimes, very seldom, a stranger came and went who had no body. He would enter one door like a picklock's knife and go out the other door. So fine he was, so insubstantial, a wind born from generations of winds. Cawdor did not see him. But he passed among Nana and the children and birds like an annunciation of dry desert and snakes and Nana smelt her soul. She loved this which was not. Then Cawdor met Nana on the dark stairs or in one of the dark high-ceilinged rooms and it seemed she was not alone. She walked like one being called from a far desert. The stranger was a poem of centerless wind. Nana knew that poem by heart. Yet there was no body there. But the stranger never stayed long. He slid into the cactus far to the south and lay there smiling, like a handsome snake.

The house closed its walls. The bottles of pills came out of their cupboards and returned. The strangers hung by the stove or sink or sat in chairs eating spinach and drinking coffee. One could trace it by dancing a circle. Nana danced the circle one way and Cawdor the other way. Occasionally they would meet in the middle of the circle and the strangers and children and birds would gather round them, it looked like a closed flower. Then Cawdor snapped the flower stem or Nana would make it wilt and the strangers faded into the walls where the shadow stood watching. The children came and went and the shadow turned itself into a child and followed them. Nana went into her dream and sat there. Cawdor lengthened World. In the silence the piano played itself. The stranger with no body lay smiling in the cactus far to the south.

Nana needed to feel. Nana did feel. But she needed to feel more. Sometimes Nana made Cawdor feel more than he needed to feel, so that two of them would feel more. Then Cawdor got angry and blamed the shadow. Until he saw Nana and the shadow together. Then he blamed Nana, because the shadow pretended to die too easily, and Cawdor needed to hit something. Nana made Cawdor feel so much that she would feel sorry for all his feelings and then their hands would touch. Nana had so much feeling that Cawdor had to shoulder much of it. Cawdor's shoulders were strong but bent. They were born strong but not bent. The more Cawdor's shoulders bent the straighter Nana stood. It was all that feeling. One felt worried about Cawdor then. One feared for Nana.

Cawdor feared for Nana. But by then Cawdor was getting tired. Cawdor feared for Cawdor. What kept Cawdor going was that he was Cawdor and should keep going. Sometimes meeting on the dark stairs Cawdor would touch Nana and the touch felt like a serpent. But Cawdor did not like serpents and therefore Nana's touch felt like a child. It might have been the shadow pretending to be Nana or a child, or it might have been Nana pretending to be a child. Cawdor was not made to see what he did not want to see. And he liked children. Between the shadow the children and Nana Cawdor was never sure. Nana was not sure either and the shadow and the shadow-in-the-children frightened her. But she knew the shadow a little and could use it to do a dance of the seven veils in front of Cawdor. She would do this with the shadow until Cawdor felt more than he needed to feel and he would attack the shadow and sometimes Nana. World lengthened and Cawdor suffered. Then Nana smiled. The children came out from behind the shadow and they all formed a ring around Nana and Cawdor and made a flower. Sometimes strangers joined the flower. It became hard to see who were the strangers. They grew so well into the flower. They lost their names or changed their names into flower names. Then Cawdor was happy and thumped his feet and danced. The shadow cringed. It was important for Cawdor to feel good.

Sometimes the children went away. They went underground and joined the ant people. They played there in whispers, Cawdor and Nana could not find them. That left Cawdor and Nana with the shadow and no children. They talked about love and the shadow joined them. They talked about cold places and hot places, the shadow had been there too. They talked as plainly as they could. But the words passed through the shadow between them and came out smoky. Nana saw the shadow in the words and Cawdor did not. Therefore the words had to be repeated over and over until the shadow let go of them. But the shadow refused. And the shadow that was in Nana's eyes, but not entirely in Nana's eyes, was not Cawdor's friend. Nana could slip through seven dreams in a single word. The shadow approved of this. The shadow did not approve of Cawdor's dictionary. World stood between Cawdor and the shadow. Sometimes Nana felt the shadow was on her side against Cawdor. Sometimes she felt Cawdor was on her side against the shadow. It depended how she felt and how she needed to feel. Sometimes Cawdor could not tell them apart. Then Nana touched his hand, and the children came back. Cawdor returned to World. The children melted into Nana as if they had not yet been born.

Cawdor rose.

Nana rose.

The children could not yet rise.

Cawdor fell with a crash.

Nana floated down like a feather.

They landed on the children. A crash and a feather. The feather hurt most. The weight of the shadow was in the feather. But one could hardly feel it. The children did. Shadow hurt them. Shadow was their friend. Shadow was Nana. Shadow was Cawdor. The children wept. Nana smiled. Cawdor smiled. The children were laughing. The strangers came out of the walls and they all made a flower.

One feared for the flower. One feared sometimes for the strangers within the flower. For the stamen and pistil in the flower were Nana and Cawdor, the rest could be plucked away. It was a curious, composite, bisexual flower. And the strangers changed their colors to be part of it. If the bee of love came to the flower, it came to Nana and Cawdor and not to the rest of the flower, the curious changeling petals, children and strangers. One sometimes longed to wring that flower's neck. It was all one so beautiful color. Yet it was not the colors of the strangers or the children or Nana and Cawdor. It was a hybrid. The strangers changed their names and altered their colors to be part of it, and when the flower broke apart they fell away with no name or color at all. They crawled into the shadow's corners and Nana and Cawdor could not find them. Then Nana or Cawdor came with soothing arms or a bandaid and the strangers and children returned. They did not quite return. Perhaps they returned a little less each time the flower wilted or fell apart. They began to see the cold eyes of the serpent in the flower, the flower they had helped to make. But the strangers with their lost names and colors did not go. The flower was the only flower they knew, they wanted to keep making it. They needed to be the flower around the pistil and stamen of Nana and Cawdor. So one worried about the strangers too.

Outside the flower it was a cold world. Even the shadow, so much at home in the world, did not want to leave. Sometimes on the dark stairs or in one of the dark high-ceilinged rooms the shadow would meet Cawdor or Nana alone. Sometimes the shadow came as an accident. Then if it was Cawdor the shadow met, it would cringe and pretend to die. If it was Nana, they would exchange eyes until the shadow wanted its eyes back. Then Nana wept and Cawdor came and again the shadow cringed and pretended to die. These were the rules for the shadow's life. It grew bored. Then the shadow would lose its head and break out and do something really unpleasant to Nana or a child. Then someone would come with soothing arms and a bandaid and it would do no good. Nana lay hidden. The children were sent to their relatives the ants, or the strangers cooked and washed and ate in silence and fed the children. Nana was gone. No flower could be made. Cawdor stormed up to World and hammered out 500 fresh cantos. Where was Nana. Where were the children. Where were the strangers. But World was lengthening. One feared for World. One feared even for the Shadow.

The shadow lay quiet. It did not dare to move. Cawdor kept going because Cawdor was Cawdor and had to keep going. There was no half Cawdor or quarter Cawdor or square root of Cawdor. But when Cawdor reached out to touch hands with Nana he touched only the shadow. Nana was gone. Nana returned. The children came back and the strangers and birds came back, softly, as if intruding. Cawdor touched Nana's hand, but it was still the shadow's hand. It was not part of the flower. The children and strangers hung from the dark walls, waiting to make a flower. But Nana's hand was not ready yet. The shadow did a sad dance, and a happy dance. The shadow looked like a child, and Nana smiled. Cawdor smiled. It was time to make a flower. Far to the south the stranger in the cactus lay smiling. One feared for the child in the shadow.

Song of the stranger smiling in the cactus

Wind has no body
sun no body
what do you seek

I have no body

you love me
I am not here

a thinness
in by one door
out by another

the cactus smiles
pricking your blood
our blood does not mingle

mirage
of the sun
far south of you   no
body
         wind has no body
         sun no body

centerless poem
the wind my cathedral

in it I starve

and am happy

The poem crept on Nana's skin like a scorpion. Cawdor met Nana on the dark stairs, and it was as if she was called from far inside herself. Cawdor touched Nana's hand. Her hand felt like cactus and desert and snakes. In the palm of her hand was the face of the stranger smiling behind the cactus. The palm of her hand was dry and across it blew a wind, hot and dry. Cawdor felt the wind and turned on the air conditioner. Nana shivered. Cawdor turned the air conditioner off. The shadow came in in the shape of a child. It walked heavily, a somnolence, unable to sleep. A stranger came bringing a plate of spinach for the child within the shadow. Nana ate it. The child in Nana was satisfied. It went up the dark stairs with the shadow following. Nana smiled. Cawdor shook out his hair and stumbled upstairs to lengthen World. The strangers became knotholes in the walls. Nana sat rocking talking to herself. The shadow slept with the children. That night Cawdor added 100 cantos to World.

Things rotted in the refrigerator and were replaced by other things. A soup boiled over, a cup of milk fell. There was love in the house, and good food. Cawdor danced the circle one way and Nana danced it the other. The strangers sometimes danced the circle too, but they got it wrong. Then Nana and Cawdor were angry. Nana forgot Cawdor was Cawdor and Cawdor forgot Nana was Nana and they became one, Nador or Cawna. In their anger. Then the strangers trembled and looked for their old names and colors but could not find them, a child got hurt and no one could find a bandaid, the soothing arms were folded, still. Then Nana told the strangers and children and birds the true story of creation, how it was. Nana was talking to herself but the house listened. Or it was the shadow talking through Nana, though not through Nana's eyes. Slowly the color and name of Nana became the strangers and children as she told them how it was. Then Nana gave the flower smile. They all got up and surrounded Nana and Cawdor and made a flower.

The sun from which Cawdor took his energy saw many people born and many injured, heard the cries of children and birds. Shadow never moved from Cawdor's house. The moon from which Nana took her energy was hidden during the day, she was left with the sun. Shadow never moved from Nana's house. The sun was too hot, the shadow was too cold.

A lot of work had gone into the house, a lot of good work. The house was big and strong. But one worried about the foundations. The house was intact. It held Nana and Cawdor and the children and strangers and the shadow like a world. But it seemed a world adrift, cut off, in orbit, or free fall. One worried about the house. One worried about the direction. Nana and Cawdor did not seem to know that the house was a house, not World. When Nana and Cawdor moved beyond the house they expected the house to follow like a dog. Nana knew about the thin stranger and the cactus and the wind but it was a film that happened inside the house. Or Nana and Cawdor knew that the house was not World, except that they did not need to feel that, so when they came to the desert they looked for the house but the house was not. So they always had to return fast to the house within the film within the shadow where Cawdor could lengthen World and Nana move from room to room each room another dream. Then it took time to dance the circle again because the circle was broken.

It took time and many strangers and children who were not the shadow pretending to be children, hurt. So Nana began to know that the stranger smiling in the cactus was not her soul. She moved, a somnolence, in search of another soul. It was not Cawdor's soul. Cawdor was laying his highway across the void. But with enough house, the desert would return again in the palm of her hand, dry wind, cactus, fang of snake. Wait.

It grew hot. It grew cold. Cawdor did not see the sun rise and set and the children pass in and out of shadow. Cawdor sat in his tower lengthening World. Occasionally Cawdor's hot eyes saw the shadow moving in a stranger, and the stranger had to cringe and pretend to die. There was love in Cawdor's house and so he wanted it. The strangers in Cawdor's house grew older and thinner and more desperate with love. They looked for their lost names and colors, under cushions, in the medicine cupboard, in discarded shoes. Perhaps Nana or the shadow or the shadow in Nana, but not entirely in Nana, knew where the names and colors were. Or the children played with the old names and colors and broke them or lost them. Nobody made the strangers stay. The strangers could not leave. They could not leave without their names and colors. Or they were afraid to break the flower. They were afraid to break the flower of love. The flower was a flower of love because it needed to be that. The strangers and children and Nana and Cawdor needed it to be that. So the shadow became a child and did a sad dance, and a happy dance. Love smiled in the flower. One worried about the love.

Song of the shadow in love

I am the shadow
in love

a child
not a child

I dance
a false flower

flower
with no shadow

I am the shadow
I dance myself

I am love of myself
not the dance, not the flower

sad dance
happy dance

of the child
between shadow and love

who eats
itself

loves
the cactus tooth

The palm of Nana's hand itched with a dry wind. Cawdor touched the hand and it was moist. Cawdor took his hand away and the itch returned. Cawdor made food. Nana ate. Her hand felt good. The food touched her hand, her hand touched the children's heads, touched Cawdor's head, his head felt good, Cawdor touched the children's heads, they touched his head, they all touched Nana's head. Everyone felt good. The strangers sat around and smiled in awe. Cawdor returned to his tower and World. The children passed upstairs with the shadow. Nana sat with the strangers and talked about love. It was important to be feeling good.

Sometimes Nana became the child within the shadow. Cawdor worried about this. Cawdor had never been a child. When Nana became the child within the shadow all the other children had to vanish and go to the ant people. When Nana became the child within the shadow Cawdor did not know what to do, he had many children and Nana was not one of them. What child was this. Then Cawdor talked to Nana as if she were a child. And Nana talked to Cawdor about the creation, how things came to be. She talked to Cawdor as if he had never been a child. One worried about the childlikeness of the shadow talking in the form of Nana being a child. Sometimes Nana needed to feel she was a child. So the shadow would let her feel she was the child within it. The shadow knew Nana was not a child. Nana knew the shadow knew she was not a child but Cawdor did not. Long ago Nana and Cawdor had agreed that Cawdor had never been a child, though not entirely never a child. Therefore when the shadow appeared as a child it was agreed that only Nana understood it and spoke for it. On those occasions Cawdor would listen respectfully while Nana explained the shadow and the child within the shadow. But there came a look about Cawdor's eyes sometimes, as if he was watching a beetle with too many legs crawl up his arm. One feared for Cawdor. Though Cawdor was strong. More and more, Cawdor had to feel good.

They would meet on the dark stairs or in one of the dark high-ceilinged rooms. Then Nana would do a sad dance, and a happy dance. Cawdor thought Nana was a beautiful child and Nana thought so too. The strangers looked as if they thought so too because they did not want to hurt the flower. It was a strong flower, though it had been a weak seed. The flower was strong because Nana and Cawdor needed it to be strong. But the flower cast no shadow. It was a hybrid, an air flower. The children were learning to make the flower. They would inherit the flower but perhaps only the petals. Nana and Cawdor did not want the hot dry desert wind to kill the flower. The thin stranger smiling in the cactus saw the flower, smiled, and went back to the desert and cactus. A rattlesnake coiled round his neck and he played with it. Nana felt the snake coil round her neck, but it was only air. Cawdor came and unwound the snake, the snake pretended to die. One of the strangers began to discourse on poison. Nana was afraid of poison and had to be led from the room. Cawdor returned. The stranger was in disgrace. The stranger cringed and pretended to die. Nana returned. Nana smiled. The stranger came out of the shadow and sat in Nana's lap. They made a plate of spinach and ate it. It was good.

Sometimes one stranger was replaced by another. Then the first stranger walked into the shadow and was not often seen again. The stranger walked away without his color and name; the color and name were forfeited to Nana and Cawdor. Because in the terms of being a stranger in the house it was unspoken but accepted that, in the event of the stranger's going, he left his name and color behind as penalty money. Then the new stranger would be given a name and color suited to his or her place in the house. The shadow watched this. With the new stranger things began as with the banished stranger. They practiced dancing the circle, this way round, that way round, and learned how to make a flower. Strangers were always replaced and always replaceable. That was because Nana and Cawdor needed there to be strangers to dance the circle and make a flower and come with a bandaid or soothing arms when a child cried or when the shadow pretending to be a child cried or when Nana pretending to be the shadow pretending to be a child, but never entirely shadow or child, wept. Also because Cawdor was often busy lengthening World in his tower and arguing with the shadow. A generation of strangers lived and died in the house. There was always love. There was always food. There was always the shadow.

Nana and Cawdor did not see the strangers dying or why they should die. Strangers were by definition something that was alive. Alive but not entirely alive, until they met Nana and Cawdor. Then their life was explained to them in several ways. When the explanation was complete the strangers forfeited their names and colors. Nana would kiss the names and colors and hide them somewhere out of reach. Nana explained the stranger's lives by explaining her own life. Cawdor explained the stranger's lives by showing them his muscles. Between the series of circles which were Nana's life and the series of circles that were Cawdor's muscles the strangers' lives were explained. Then the male strangers danced Cawdor's half of the circle, the female strangers danced Nana's half of the circle, they all made a flower, and the flower was good. But the strangers never quite got the circle right. When that happened Nana wept, Cawdor thumped his feet and did an angry dance. The strangers cringed and pretended to die. The shadow followed the children off into dark high-ceilinged distant rooms. The children did a sad dance, and a happy dance. Or it was Nana at the piano. The house felt bad.

How did the strangers get there. The strangers were brought by Cawdor who was the only one who really left the house and knew about World. Cawdor brought the strangers back like kill and gave them to Nana. Then Nana explained herself to the strangers and that was their own explanation too. On these occasions Nana was very happy. The children came and the birds and admired the stranger. The stranger admired the children the birds and Nana. As soon as possible they made a flower. As soon as possible the stranger cooked and washed and ate and fed the children and came with a bandaid or soothing arms if a child looked hurt or was lost somewhere in the shadow. Then Nana would explain the shadow to the stranger. She borrowed the shadow's eyes to do it then gave them back. New strangers were immune to the shadow. There was a tree Cawdor planted in the yard, a young sapling. This tree was Nana's. The strangers were taken to the tree. Once the tree was dying. Cawdor bore down on the tree with all his energy, and the tree leafed and pretended to live.

Song of the tree pretending to live

O death
under the sun

between the winds
water me

an old race
weakens in my seed
too hot, too cold

I was patient
and needed time

I am not given time
but forced from your hands

with care and water like
a scar kissed to life
too quick, too late

leave me to die or grow
my own way
along my roots

your dark house
needs no shadow of mine
I mistrust your hands

Day rose and fell. The song of the tree pretending to live did not reach Nana or Cawdor. Nana and Cawdor needed the tree to live. They needed the little tree to feel like them and need to live. If the tree lived Nana and Cawdor accepted it as part of the dance and the flower, the children the birds and strangers. If the tree died then it was hostile. If it died it walked into the shadow and was never mentioned again. So the tree remained outside and sang its death song. Inside nothing ever sang a death song. Nana and Cawdor were afraid of death songs, it was agreed that Nana should never be made to hear a death song. If Nana did she wept and had to be led from the room. When Cawdor returned whatever had sung the death song cringed and pretended to die. Strangers who knew death songs never lasted long. Perhaps the thin stranger smiling in the cactus knew this.

One by one the children entered the shadow. It was hard to tell shadow and child apart. World lengthened and sometimes Nana thought she knew the shadow and sometimes she knew she did not. Nana exchanged eyes with the shadow, but the shadow kept Nana's eyes much longer now. With the shadow's eyes Nana could see very far. But it hurt her. Her sockets ached from wearing the shadow's eyes. Then Cawdor came back from World. He tried, very reasonably, to get the shadow to give Nana back her eyes. But the shadow played tricks. Sometimes it would not give Nana back her own eyes but the eyes of a child or in extreme moments the eyes of a stranger. Then Nana screamed and Cawdor attacked the shadow and the shadow cringed and pretended to die but still with Nana's eyes. Then Cawdor thumped the shadow with all his might and Nana's eyes came back, worn and tired and very frightened.

The walls were dented with marks of Cawdor's fists. Then a child came out of the shadow with many bruises. For it was hard to tell shadow and child apart. Then Cawdor or Nana or a stranger came with a bandaid or soothing arms or a plate of spinach for the child. The shadow ate the food and was grateful. Or the child ate the food, it was hard to tell. Or Nana ate the food. If Nana ate the food she smiled, and the children and strangers crept into her lap. Then Cawdor returned to World and hammered out 200 new cantos. One feared for everything.

Everything feared for itself. The tree sang its death song and was afraid. The children in the shadow or the shadow in the children or the shadow become the children were afraid. The strangers were afraid and hunted everywhere for their lost names and colors. Nana and Cawdor were afraid but they did not need to feel afraid so they pretended they were not afraid and were not afraid, much. Only the stranger smiling in the cactus far to the south was not afraid. He had no body.

Cawdor lived in his World. World was whatever he could get his hands on. World was whatever he could get his hands on that was not him, but that could become him if he exerted all his energy and bore down on it. As long as Cawdor had World there was no shadow in Cawdor's World. So World lengthened at the rate of 500 cantos a day on a good day and 700 cantos a day on a bad day. More on a bad day because then Cawdor had to lengthen World to keep out the shadow or the children within the shadow who were becoming the shadow itself or Nana pretending to be the shadow or a child within the shadow becoming the shadow itself. On those days the house was full of the shadow wearing Nana's eyes or Nana wearing the shadow's eyes which were sometimes the eyes of a child or even the eyes of a stranger. Then Cawdor smote World with all his might. World really belonged to others. But when Cawdor smote World World became Cawdor's. World became Cawdor's because Cawdor needed it to become his, he did not need to feel that World was not his. So the tree sang its death song, and the others who were part of World sang their death songs, but Cawdor smote World and did not hear the death songs. A generation of insects lived and died outside the windows of the house. Nana moved in and out of shadow, like a dark flashlight. Cawdor heard. Cawdor met Nana on the stairs or in one of the dark high-ceilinged rooms. Then Nana would do a sad dance, and a happy dance. And Cawdor saw Nana as a beautiful child. But sometimes Cawdor saw Nana as the shadow pretending to be Nana pretending to be a beautiful child, though a not entirely beautiful child. Then Cawdor stumbled upstairs and lengthened World. It was great and noble. But where was Cawdor.

Where was anyone. There was the shadow. The shadow was no one. The shadow was becoming the children and the strangers and Nana. So long as Cawdor was lengthening World the shadow could not become Cawdor. What Cawdor really feared was when World could no longer be lengthened. Then there would be Nana the children the strangers. The shadow. Cawdor. No World. Sometimes Cawdor thought about the shadow.

Song of Cawdor thinking about the shadow

I was born within you
I wanted out
I got out

you were my mother
my father
I hate and love

you do not exist

you are the eyes
of my children
I do not see my children's eyes

I am the world
in sunlight
I do not see the dark world
in my children's eyes

I do not see you

I see you through others
who found you,
her, dead men
and women

they are not part
of my house
my house is World

the tree must live

I have gathered these voices
against you

they are not mine

that World survive

in me

Then Cawdor returned to World. His own voice did not put fear enough into the shadow. Nana's voice was the shadow. Nana's voice was sometimes the children's eyes. The shadow began to give and take eyes indiscriminately. Sometimes the strangers felt a pain in their eyes and looked up and they were blind. Then Nana smiled and gave them back their eyes and no one thought this was strange. Then there would be an eye-exchanging party in which everyone took everyone else's eyes and did a sad dance, and a happy dance. Then whoever wound up the game with children's eyes was kissed by Nana and sat in her lap. Then everyone would rub their eyes and agree that Nana was a beautiful child. Everyone would agree that they were neither beautiful nor had ever been children, compared with Nana. Then they would make a flower, like an adoration. Nana loved it and hated it. To Nana it was both pleasure and pain. Perhaps it was all the same. One worried about the sameness of the pleasure and pain.

Cawdor did not. Pain was alive. Pleasure was being alive with pain. Only shadow was like death and was dangerous. A point of rest. Where. Strangers came with bandaids or soothing arms and all they found were the walls. Walls were the shadow pretending to be a child or already become one. A child with Nana's eyes staring at the walls looking for a child that should have been hers but was no longer because the knotholes contained strangers who were becoming the shadow too. Cawdor thumped the walls and Nana heard the screams of her children who were Cawdor's too. Cawdor thumped the walls until they screamed and the cry was a shadow. Then Cawdor approached the shadow with a bandaid and soothing arms and the shadow had Nana's eyes which were weeping. Cawdor dried the eyes and found they were a stranger's. A child came and took the eyes who gave them back to Nana who in turn asked the shadow for hers but they were a stranger's. The shadow laughed. It was a mistake. Cawdor found the shadow and thumped it with all his might. The shadow was in possession of all the eyes. They were bruised, every one. That night no one had eyes. Feebly they made a blind flower, but it was not good. They made a plate of spinach but it got burnt. Only Cawdor had his eyes. The shadow did not have his eyes because he did not see it. Cawdor was lengthening World. His eyes were laying a highway across a void.

By now the shadow had many bodies. By now the shadow also had many bruises. Nana and Cawdor argued about whose bodies the shadow had. Cawdor said he was in full possession of his body. Nana said she was not and nor were the children let alone the strangers who had neither name nor color and perhaps were the shadow anyhow. Nana and Cawdor talked about love and how could the children do this to them. How could the strangers. Then Cawdor would say very reasonably that the strangers were strangers and the children were children, though not entirely children and strangers he agreed. Then Nana told Cawdor the story of creation, how it was. Nana did this by explaining her own life which also explained the world. When she did this Nana resembled a beautiful child, though not entirely beautiful and not entirely a child. Cawdor would listen quietly, bathing in Nana's eyes like a little boy swimming in a swimming hole. Children would come tiptoeing up like deer, then the strangers. Soon there would be a flower. Nana smiled. The children would be forgiven. The strangers within the shadow within the children would be forgiven.

Nana's song of creation, how it was

Chick
born in a snowdrift
child of the sick eagle

I burn in the cold
I have no body

my eyes
are the snow's eyes
melting and hardening

I know the way in
I know no way out

empty
        empty
but pain is not empty

pain is the
full sun
to the drowned

the snow-drowned
the cold infected
the eaten by ice

but I returned
to survive

strong teeth
and pink fleshy wings
but moon-confused

clear
and hidden

afraid of my blood
afraid of all blood
no love but my own

I am here to tell you
how it began

how it ends

Then Nana was led from the room, softly, by Cawdor. The song hung in the air between the four walls. The night insects sent their voices in but the song rebuffed them. The strangers gathered the children and moved gently so as not to hurt the song through the room and up the dark stairs to their beds. When everyone had left the room the shadow snatched the song and ate it up. There was always shadow in the house. There was always a song to feed it. One worried about the way the shadow fattened on songs.

By now no one knew how anyone felt because nobody was anybody. Cawdor mistook Nana for strangers and Nana mistook Cawdor for the shadow who had never been a child and wished to be a child. The children had gone far into the shadow, or were the shadow. Strangers sometimes looked like the children or looked like Nana or Cawdor in a bad light. So Cawdor decided that no one should wear any clothes. Nana and Cawdor took off their clothes. The children took off their clothes, the strangers took off their clothes. Perhaps the shadow had been hiding in their clothes. Naked was better. Nana liked being naked. It made her feel a child. Cawdor liked being naked. It made him feel a bull. They all felt closer to children. And the closer they felt to being children the harder it was for the shadow to be a child or a stranger or Nana. Perhaps the shadow was in Cawdor too and they did not know it. Cawdor felt in his bush and touched his balls and backside. No shadow. Nana smiled. Nana felt in Cawdor's bush and touched his balls and backside. No shadow. The strangers and children felt in Cawdor's bush and touched his balls and backside. It felt unusual. But they could find no shadow. So Cawdor widened the big bed and Cawdor and Nana and the strangers and children all went to bed together. Cawdor slept with the strangers one by one then he slept with Nana. Then Nana slept with the strangers one by one and then with Cawdor. They did not sleep with the children because the children were not up to it yet. Then the strangers thanked Nana and Cawdor, and in the morning they all wept and talked about love. Still no one knew how anyone felt because nobody was anybody. No one knew who anyone was. No one was feeling good.

The bandaids were lost. The children fell, hurt, and were not soothed. Naked or clothed, the shadow had stolen the children. Cawdor lengthened World. Nana watched World lengthen and cried to Cawdor to stop. Nana had words Cawdor did not have. A stranger slept with Cawdor. A stranger slept with Nana or with the shadow pretending to be Nana or perhaps the stranger was the dry desert wind coiled like a snake between her legs. Slowly the strangers became the shadow too.

The shadow slept with Nana. Cawdor slept with the shadow who was a stranger without knowing the stranger was the shadow. The shadow thanked Cawdor and Cawdor slept with Nana. Nana thanked the shadow, and they made a flower in the bed. In the morning they drank coffee ate spinach and wept, talking about love. The shadow did a sad dance, and a happy dance. Sometimes the shadow looked like Nana. Sometimes, now, the shadow looked like Cawdor.

The strangers left. But there would always be strangers. The strangers left because the shadow ate them. Sometimes the strangers came back, but it was only their bones. The shadow did not eat the children yet. The shadow had other plans. There were always strangers.

Now Nana and Cawdor fought. Each in his and her heart was making a noose to hang the other. But they talked about love. They talked about love which meant death but no one sang a death song. Nana and Cawdor could go on forever talking about love which meant death without singing a death song. Because neither Nana nor Cawdor needed to hear a death song when what they really meant was love. Love of Nana. Love of Cawdor. Love of children. Love of strangers. Death to all. Death to all but Nana. Death to all but Cawdor. Death to all. The shadow pricked up its ears. It was not hearing right. It was not time yet. One feared for the timing of the shadow's plans.

But it was not over. Cawdor did not want it over. Nana did not want it over. There were always strangers. There were always the children. They stood naked, day rose and fell on a house without windows. World lengthened. Cawdor laid his highway across the void. Nana moved, a somnolence, in the shadow. It had to break. It would not break. The shadow refused to go. The shadow was no one and everyone. Nana moved, a darkened torch, across the face of Cawdor's clock that had no hands. They slept with the wind. They slept with serpent and cactus. They could not find the smiling stranger. They could find no one. But themselves. Wherever they went they would find no one but themselves. For they had to feel they were selves more than others felt it. That was the shadow's plan. So they opened the door to new strangers. Not here perhaps, but somewhere else, the door opened.

Song of the new strangers at the open door

I see light
I see welcoming eyes
of the sun and the moon in love

it is too hot outside
too hot or too cold

we come as bones
perhaps we will leave as bones

cherish us   cherish us
our names our colors are dying

you who have none be our lovers
take us
take us

TAVERN BOOKS

Tavern Books is a not-for-profit poetry publisher that exists to print, promote, and preserve works of literary vision, to foster a climate of cultural preservation, and to disseminate books in a way that benefits the reading public.

We publish books in translation from the world's finest poets, champion new works by innovative writers, and revive of out-of-print classics. We keep our titles in print, honoring the cultural contract between publisher and author, as well as between publisher and public. Our catalog, known as The Living Library, sustains the visions of our authors, ensuring their voices remain alive in the social and artistic discourse of our modern era.

THE LIVING LIBRARY

Arthur's Talk with the Eagle by Anonymous,
translated from the Welsh by Gwyneth Lewis

Ashulia by Zubair Ahmed

Breckinridge County Suite by Joe Bolton

My People & Other Poems by Wojciech Bonowicz,
translated from the Polish by Piotr Florczyk

Buson: Haiku by Yosa Buson,
translated from the Japanese by Franz Wright

Evidence of What Is Said by Ann Charters and Charles Olson

Who Whispered Near Me by Killarney Clary

The End of Space by Albert Goldbarth

Six-Minute Poems: The Last Poems
by George Hitchcock

The Wounded Alphabet: Collected Poems
by George Hitchcock

Hitchcock on Trial
by George Hitchcock

My Blue Piano by Else Lasker-Schüler,
translated from the German by Eavan Boland

Why We Live in the Dark Ages by Megan Levad

Archeology by Adrian C. Louis

Fire Water World & Among the Dog Eaters
by Adrian C. Louis

Emergency Brake by Ruth Madievsky

Under an Arkansas Sky by Jo McDougall

The Undiscovered Room by Jo McDougall

Ocean by Joseph Millar

Petra by Amjad Nasser,
translated from the Arabic by Fady Joudah

The Fire's Journey: Part I by Eunice Odio,
translated from the Spanish by Keith Ekiss
with Sonia P. Ticas and Mauricio Espinoza

The Fire's Journey: Part II by Eunice Odio,
translated from the Spanish by Keith Ekiss
with Sonia P. Ticas and Mauricio Espinoza

*The Fire's Journey: Part III by Eunice Odio,
translated from the Spanish by Keith Ekiss
with Sonia P. Ticas and Mauricio Espinoza

*The Fire's Journey: Part IV by Eunice Odio,
translated from the Spanish by Keith Ekiss
with Sonia P. Ticas and Mauricio Espinoza

Duino Elegies by Rainer Maria Rilke,
translated from the German by Gary Miranda

Twelve Poems about Cavafy by Yannis Ritsos,
translated from the Greek by Paul Merchant

Glowing Enigmas by Nelly Sachs,
translated from the German by Michael Hamburger

Prodigy by Charles Simic,
drawings by Charles Seluzicki

Night of Shooting Stars by Leonardo Sinisgalli,
translated from the Italian by W. S. Di Piero

Skin by Tone Škrjanec,
translated from the Slovene by Matthew Rohrer and Ana Pepelnik

We Women by Edith Södergran,
translated from the Swedish by Samuel Charters

Building the Barricade by Anna Świrszczyńska,
translated from the Polish by Piotr Florczyk

Baltics by Tomas Tranströmer
with photographs by Ann Charters,
translated from the Swedish by Samuel Charters

For the Living and the Dead by Tomas Tranströmer,
translated from the Swedish by John F. Deane

Prison by Tomas Tranströmer
with a postscript by Jonas Ellerström,
translated from the Swedish by Malena Mörling

Where the Arrow Falls by David Wevill

Collected Translations by David Wevill

Night Is Simply a Shadow by Greta Wrolstad

Notes on Sea & Shore by Greta Wrolstad

The Countries We Live In by Natan Zach,
translated from the Hebrew by Peter Everwine

*forthcoming

Tavern Books is funded, in part, by the generosity of philanthropic organizations, public and private institutions, and individual donors. By supporting Tavern Books and its mission, you enable us to publish the most exciting poets from around the world. To learn more about underwriting Tavern Books titles, please contact us by e-mail: info@tavernbooks.org.

MAJOR FUNDING HAS BEEN PROVIDED BY

THE PUBLICATION OF THIS BOOK IS MADE POSSIBLE,
IN PART, BY THE SUPPORT OF THE FOLLOWING INDIVIDUALS

Gabriel Boehmer
Dean & Karen Garyet
Mark Swartz & Jennifer Jones
The Mancini Family
Mary Ann Ryan
Marjorie Simon

Donna Swartz
Mary Szybist & Jerry Harp
Bill & Leah Stenson
Vince & Patty Wixon
Ron & Kathy Wrolstad

SUBSCRIPTIONS

Become a subscriber and receive the next six Tavern Books titles at a substantial discount, delivered to your door. Paperback and hardcover subscriptions available.

For details visit www.tavernbooks.org or write to us at:

Tavern Books
at Union Station
800 NW 6th Avenue #255
Portland, Oregon 97209

COLOPHON

This book was designed and typeset by Eldon Potter at Bryan Potter Design, Portland, Oregon. Text is set in Garamond, an old-style serif typeface named for the punch-cutter Claude Garamond (c. 1480-1561). Display font is Bluescreens, a cinema-inspired typeface designed by Ivan Gladkikh. *Where the Arrow Falls* appears in both paperback and cloth-covered editions. Printed on archival-quality paper by McNaughton & Gunn, Inc.